BUT THIS NIGHT
IS DIFFERENT

Audrey Friedman Marcus • Raymond A. Zwerin

BUT THIS NIGHT IS DIFFERENT

A Seder Experience

Illustrated by JUDITH GWYN BROWN

Union of American Hebrew Congregations

Library of Congress Catalog Card Number: 80-68979
ISBN 0-8074-0032-7

Manufactured in the United States of America

2 3 4 5 6 7 8 9 0

This series of holiday books for young children
dedicated to Mildred and Matthew H. Ross
is made possible by
The Blum Family Publication Fund

Max and the late Ida
Helene and the late Sidney

To Julius ז״ל and Anne Ritter and
to Irwin and Mary Zwerin
our parents,
at whose tables we learned that life has
both order and questions

Why is this night different?

It begins just like other holidays.

BUT THIS NIGHT IS DIFFERENT.

On most nights we just sit down and eat.
BUT THIS NIGHT IS DIFFERENT.
On this night we first share stories and prayers.

On other nights we wash our hands at the sink.

BUT THIS NIGHT IS DIFFERENT.
On this night we wash our hands at the table.

On Shabbat and other holidays
we say Kiddush and drink the wine only once.
BUT THIS NIGHT IS DIFFERENT.

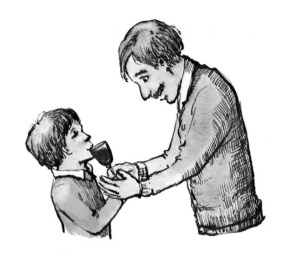

On this night we say Kiddush and sip
sweet wine four different times.

On other nights we ask all kinds of questions.
BUT THIS NIGHT IS DIFFERENT.

On this night we always ask four special questions.

Many times we eat without telling stories.
BUT THIS NIGHT IS DIFFERENT.
On this night we always tell the story of Exodus.

We remember what happened to the Jewish people
in Egypt long ago.

We remember that there was a cruel pharaoh.

We remember that we were his slaves.

We remember how Moses led us out of Egypt.

MY
CAT

At other times we show and tell at school.
BUT THIS NIGHT IS DIFFERENT.

זְרֹועַ
Zeroa

כַּרְפַּס
Karpas

מָרוֹר
Maror

salt and water

בֵּיצָה
Betzah

חֲרֹסֶת
Charoset

On this night we show and tell at home.

All through the year we eat soft, chewy bread.
BUT THIS NIGHT IS DIFFERENT.

On this night we eat hard, crunchy matzah.

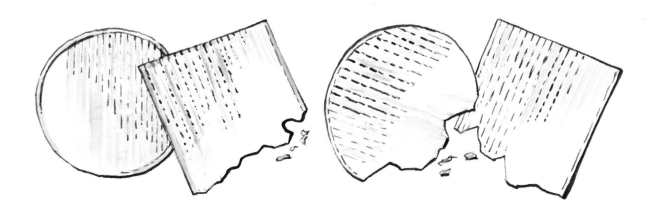

parsley

We don't usually dip our food in anything at the table.
BUT THIS NIGHT IS DIFFERENT.
On this night we dip two things, karpas and maror.

We all make many kinds of sandwiches.
BUT THIS NIGHT IS DIFFERENT.
On this night we all make a Hillel sandwich.

horseradish

We often thank God for lots of things.
BUT THIS NIGHT IS DIFFERENT.
On this night we thank God especially for freedom.

On other nights we may say a few blessings.
BUT THIS NIGHT IS DIFFERENT.
On this night we say many blessings.

BLESSINGS

Candles

בָּרוּךְ אַתָּה יְיָ אֱלֹהֵינוּ מֶלֶךְ הָעוֹלָם אֲשֶׁר קִדְּשָׁנוּ בְּמִצְוֹתָיו וְצִוָּנוּ
לְהַדְלִיק נֵר שֶׁל יוֹם טוֹב.

Baruch Atah Adonai, Eloheinu Melech ha'olam, asher kideshanu bemitzvotav
vetzivanu lehadlik ner shel Yom Tov.

Wine (Kiddush)

בָּרוּךְ אַתָּה יְיָ אֱלֹהֵינוּ מֶלֶךְ הָעוֹלָם בּוֹרֵא פְּרִי הַגָּפֶן.

Baruch Atah Adonai, Eloheinu Melech ha'olam, borei peri hagafen.

Karpas

בָּרוּךְ אַתָּה יְיָ אֱלֹהֵינוּ מֶלֶךְ הָעוֹלָם בּוֹרֵא פְּרִי הָאֲדָמָה.

Baruch Atah Adonai, Eloheinu Melech ha'olam, borei peri ha'adamah.

Hand washing

בָּרוּךְ אַתָּה יְיָ אֱלֹהֵינוּ מֶלֶךְ הָעוֹלָם אֲשֶׁר קִדְּשָׁנוּ בְּמִצְוֹתָיו וְצִוָּנוּ עַל
נְטִילַת יָדָיִם.

Baruch Atah Adonai, Eloheinu Melech ha'olam, asher kideshanu bemitzvotav
vetzivanu al netilat yadayim.

Motzi

בָּרוּךְ אַתָּה יְיָ אֱלֹהֵינוּ מֶלֶךְ הָעוֹלָם הַמּוֹצִיא לֶחֶם מִן הָאָרֶץ.

Baruch Atah Adonai, Eloheinu Melech ha'olam, hamotzi lechem min ha'aretz.

Matzah

בָּרוּךְ אַתָּה יְיָ אֱלֹהֵינוּ מֶלֶךְ הָעוֹלָם אֲשֶׁר קִדְּשָׁנוּ בְּמִצְוֹתָיו וְצִוָּנוּ עַל
אֲכִילַת מַצָּה.

Baruch Atah Adonai, Eloheinu Melech ha'olam, asher kideshanu bemitzvotav
vetzivanu al achilat matzah.

Maror

בָּרוּךְ אַתָּה יְיָ אֱלֹהֵינוּ מֶלֶךְ הָעוֹלָם אֲשֶׁר קִדְּשָׁנוּ בְּמִצְוֹתָיו וְצִוָּנוּ עַל
אֲכִילַת מָרוֹר.

Baruch Atah Adonai, Eloheinu Melech ha'olam, asher kideshanu bemitzvotav
vetzivanu al achilat maror.

At other times we may sing songs.
BUT THIS NIGHT IS DIFFERENT.
On this night we always sing the special Pesach songs.

During the year we sometimes play hide-and-seek.
BUT THIS NIGHT IS DIFFERENT.

On this night we hide and seek the Afikoman.

We usually open the door when
the doorbell rings.
BUT THIS NIGHT IS DIFFERENT.

On this night we open the door at a special time.
We hope Elijah is there.

On all other nights we have many feelings.
BUT THIS NIGHT IS DIFFERENT.
On this night we feel especially close to our family
and friends. We feel especially Jewish.

All year long we wish for many good things.
BUT THIS NIGHT IS DIFFERENT.
On this night we wish for the Jewish people:
Next Year in Jerusalem!

לְשָׁנָה הַבָּאָה בִּירוּשָׁלָיִם!

Leshanah Habaah Birushalayim!

Other nights may not be too exciting.
BUT THIS NIGHT IS DIFFERENT.
On this night we

SAY Kiddush and sip sweet wine four times
DIP two things, karpas and maror
EAT hard, crunchy matzah
ASK four special questions
TELL the story of Exodus
REMEMBER what happened to the Jewish people
in Egypt long ago
WASH our hands at the table
THANK God especially for freedom
SHOW the Seder plate and tell about the Pesach symbols
MAKE a Hillel sandwich
SAY many blessings
SHARE the stories and prayers
HIDE and seek the Afikoman
OPEN the door for Elijah
SING the special Pesach songs
WISH for the Jewish people
FEEL close to our family and feel especially Jewish.

About the Authors

Among their occupations and many activities, AUDREY FRIED-MAN MARCUS is the creator of *Alternatives* magazine and a well-known consultant and workshop leader and RAYMOND A. ZWERIN is the founding rabbi of Temple Sinai in Denver and author of the UAHC textbook *For One Another*. Whether separately or together—as partners in their own publishing company, Alternatives in Religious Education, Inc., or as the authors of *Shabbat Can Be*, UAHC, 1979—they are known and respected for their innovative approach to Jewish education. Their numerous books and games are the delight of Jewish children everywhere.

But This Night Is Different: A Seder Experience continues their warm celebration of Jewish tradition.

About the Artist

JUDITH GWYN BROWN, illustrator, portraitist, and the author of *Alphabet Dreams* (1976), serves on the Committee for the Picture Collection of the New York Public Library and is a member of the committee's board of directors. Her illustrations, for a widely diversified number of children's books, reflect many moods and events. *But This Night Is Different* is Miss Brown's first work for the Union of American Hebrew Congregations.

Some Very Special People

Dr. Jack Horowitz, Zena Sulkes, Alan Waldman,
Rabbi Joel Wittstein, Rabbi Daniel B. Syme,
Rabbi Steven M. Reuben, Ralph Davis, Stuart L. Benick